# Praise for #Next Level Manners

"I am so excited about this book and its approach to an important topic. I want this book in the hands of every millennial who wants to blaze a trail. Over and over again I see my talented and intelligent millennials enter the workplace and run into unexpected challenges. It turns out that activating their manners, next level manners that is, can be a powerful tool for business success."

—Dr. Ellen Ensher, Professor of Human Resource Management, Loyola Marymount University

"Love the illustrations. They make the book rich and interesting. The characters and situations make me LOL."

—Catherine Abraham, New Media Producer

"Millennials will find this book very useful. It is an easy way to learn proper business etiquette, which is an important step for anyone's career development."

—Greg Dawley, Investment Banker

# # NEXT LEVEL MANNERS

# # NEXT LEVEL MANNERS

## Business Etiquette for Millennials

**Rachel Isgar, Ph.D.**
**Illustrated by Sarah Lane**

PLEASE
PASS THE MANNERS
www.pleasepassthemanners.com

Published by Please Pass the Manners
http://pleasepassthemanners.com/nextlevelmanners

Printed in the United States of America

Cover Design by Sarah Lane
Illustrations by Sarah Lane

ISBN: 978-0-692-88777-6
ISBN: 978-0-692-88778-3 (ebook)

For Charlie, Lizzy, Chuck, Ally, and Caroline.
Thank you for inspiring me every day!

# Contents

# The Next Level of Your Success

*#Next Level Manners* is not about being prim and proper. In fact, I know you don't need or want a traditional etiquette handbook. The way I see it is that in today's world, business etiquette is about raising the bar on your personal brand. What you need is a "manners toolbox" to help you build your #Next Level Success.

It makes sense—having a solid set of manners at hand will give you a basic strategy for the type of interactions that will raise that bar. The right business etiquette will make you stand out in all kind of great ways.

As a #Millennial you can argue that others don't have good manners, and you don't need them either. You can argue that it is a new type of workplace, more casual and with a go-with-the-flow attitude. You can argue all you want . . . while watching your career success stall and your personal brand head downhill.

Or you can next level your manners.

The work world is an unpredictable place. You would think that, if you are the greatest coder, blogger, or videographer in the company, or if you are a social media marketing master, those skills would be enough to cement your success in place. But the people who inhabit those workplaces will also want face-to-face communication and this is exactly where your ascent up the company ladder can stall. Don't let this happen to you. Instead, use the "tools" in this book and build your personal brand.

Ultimately, #Next Level Manners are about the people you interact with feeling respected and acknowledged, because no matter the formality level of your workplace and/or field, being able to make others feel respected and acknowledged is a winning strategy. It will be super easy, effective, and rewarding.

Although I admit that this is a book about business etiquette for millennials, I am not going to stereotype you and talk to you about manners as if I was your mother. I would rather we get on the same page, and talk about how #Next Level Manners will next level your career. Now that's what I am talking about.

# Tweet, Text, & Post

If you do all of your communication online and in social media but neglect face-to-face time with your colleagues and/or clients, your personal brand marks will be registering on the low side. If you communicate with your colleagues via apps and social media while sitting in the same room, your personal brand will hit the floor.

There is even a new psychological term to cover our addiction to our electronic devices: FOMO (Fear of Missing Out). The statistics are compelling. Studies show us that the average person checks his/her phone almost 50 times per day. Those between the ages of 18 and 24 check their phones between 80 and 90 times a day.

The first thing to recognize is that in order to next level your success, you need not just to communicate online but also face-to-face. And when you do communicate face-to-face, you will need to put your electronic devices down and fully engage with the person or people with you. This will be harder than you think, because most of you are addicted to your electronics. But it is also true that raising the bar on your communication skills will cement a great personal impression.

It will take discipline to put your beloved device down. Furthermore, you will need not just to put your device down but also out of sight. If you can see it, you will want to check it. You will think you can check it quickly and that no one will notice, but they will notice. You will lose your eye contact with the person who is speaking. That person will see your focus shift away from what s/he is saying. Everyone around you is likely to be offended. The message you will be sending is that your Facebook feed or Twitter tweets are more important than the people you are communicating with face-to-face.

Meanwhile, when you are online, you also want to up your game by tweeting, texting, and posting in the most fleek ways—so your manners matter. You really have to think about what you share and how you share it. You want to slay all the ways you communicate online. Follow the suggestions in this section and you will be well on your way to next leveling your success!

## Top Ten Guidelines   *for tweeting, texting, & posting*

1. Silence can be golden, so turn off the ringer on your phones and iPads.
2. Don't always have the last word. It has to end sometime, but let the person know you are ending if you are ready to exit. Don't blow them off cold.
3. Think and think some more before you post business stuff on your personal accounts.
4. Leave your boss out of your personal social media loop.
5. Don't overshare online.
6. Don't cyberbully anyone, anywhere, anytime.
7. Don't communicate with work colleagues and bosses late at night. There are business hours, even in the cyberworld.
8. Emojis are for fun not work—unless you work at an emoji company.
9. Don't be the online town crier—your friends don't need hourly news reports.
10. In all your online communication, use your spell check and be careful about who is included in your reply or cc line.

# #Time Out

At the beginning of many business meetings, all the smart phones are collected in a bowl and stay there until the end of the meeting. This takes away the temptation to answer a call, check your texts, send an email, play a game, . . . (the potential distractions go on and on).

If the "device bowl" is not a feature at your company, at least put your phone and/or tablet into a metaphorical bowl and turn off any notification sounds. Be a leader; let the group know you are going unplugged. You do not want to be the one with the ringing phone just as your CEO or a most valued colleague starts to speak. Putting it away will also render it "safe" from your curiosity about who is calling, texting, or sending you funny Snapchats.

## Silence is Golden—Going Unplugged is Hard

Thanks to addictive smart phones and electronic devices, millennials are the most distracted generation. Are you addicted to your smartphone? We can't say we are not distracted when on average we touch (tap, type, swipe, and click) our devices 2,617 times per day, according to a study by research firm Dscout. If you are addicted, check out BreakFree, an app you can download to get your personal stats.

During a meeting, with one person or many, follow these golden rules:

- The best mode for your phone/tablet is "off."
- Definitely silence your notifications during formal meetings or when someone is performing or presenting.
- Choosing "silent" mode during any face-to-face interaction, even in informal situations, is also a great idea, one that allows you to focus your attention on the person/people you are with.
- If on "silent" or "off," you will not be able to hear your phone/tablet—don't then fall into the trap of continuously checking it.
- In fact, it is best to keep your phone in your pocket/purse and out of sight—not on the table or in your hand. If your hand feels lonely, grab a pen.

# Special Circumstances Are Special

Sometimes you can't avoid using a phone during meetings. During these circumstances, follow the best practices outlined here.

## *"Need to Answer" Situations*

There are times when you are expecting an important incoming call, text, or message and need to respond to it in a timely manner. One example might be if you're waiting for a call from your doctor or boss.

Let the people you are with know the situation beforehand so they understand why your device is out. Turn off the sound on your phone but put it in vibrate mode or set it on the table where you can see that a call, text, or message is coming in.

If and when that call, text, or message comes in, take your phone outside the room where you are meeting and answer it. If you are just standing in the hallway near the room, be careful about talking too loudly, and definitely don't use speaker mode.

## *Using Your Device for the Meeting*

You might be using your phone or tablet to take notes or photos during a meeting or presentation. If so, make sure the device is in silent mode and let the appropriate people know that you are using your phone or tablet for the meeting, not as a distraction from the meeting.

If you need someone to use a phone or tablet to look up information for the meeting, you might want to designate a "Googler" instead of having everyone jump in with an excuse to check their messages.

If someone is late to a meeting, don't have everyone spend time tracking that person's ETA (Estimated Time of Arrival). If the person is crucial to the meeting, designate one person to find out what is going on. The best choice is for all of you to focus your attention on the meeting.

**TIP #1:** You are not that important. Don't become the distraction in the room. Unplug from all of your electronic devices.

**TIP #2:** If your itch is to look at your screen, you need to pocket it. Find something else to fidget with. Stay unplugged for the whole meeting!

# #Social Media

You are probably already using the professional networking sites such as LinkedIn as well as social networking sites such as Facebook and SnapChat. Add in Twitter, Instagram, Pinterest, and others, and you have an ever-evolving social media landscape.

The important point to social media is that what you do there can be very visible, and this visibility could easily spread to your work colleagues and clients—even if you are posting on a personal account. These days, it can definitely be difficult to maintain a filter between your personal posts and your professional life. On social media, they tend to blend together.

Remember, your use of social media can have real consequences. In CareerBuilder surveys, 18 percent of employers report the firing of employees for posting inappropriate material on social media. Employees also get fired for personal use of the Internet during working hours. According to CareerBuilder, 28 percent of employers have fired workers for this reason.

On the other hand, you can make this work to your advantage, by using your #Next Level Manners in both your personal and professional postings. Let your social media personal brand add to your professional success.

## Think Before You Post

We have all heard the stories. Once something is posted online, it will always be out there, whether or not you delete it, because even if just one person takes a screen shot, it can then be shared and take on a life of its own. And what is out there about you will affect your personal brand. You want what is posted to boost your success, not kill it.

Naturally, you do not have complete control over what is posted about you, but if you are careful not to post embarrassing things about others, the bet is that they will not post embarrassing things about you. This will save everyone a lot of grief.

Here are some tips for posting:

- Never post
  - Anything you would not want your boss to see.
  - Anything that will embarrass someone else.
  - Rants about work-related issues.
  - Brags about how much you can drink and party.
- Track your privacy settings. Instead of worrying about how many likes you are getting, pay attention to your settings. Know who can see your posts.
- Tag with care.
- If the photo does not flatter someone, ask yourself how you would feel if a friend posted and tagged a similar photo of you. When in doubt, don't post the photo. Keep your life simple.
- Do not tag someone if he/she is not actually in the photo (unless you have that person's permission).
- Think through any unfriending, unfollowing, etc.
  - Once you have thought about unfriending or unfollowing someone—think again. If you are upset or angry, wait until you cool down. These actions are impossible to retract once implemented. Always wait a few hours to regroup and reevaluate.
  - The best time to unfriend is when there has been a gap in engagement to make it less personal.
- The big question: Do you friend/follow/connect to your boss? Think, and think again, before hitting that particular button—when in doubt, don't!
- If you are working on a post for the whole world, test it with a friend first.

Here are some tips on using emojis:

- First and foremost, follow your company's policy.
- Limit your use of emojis on business communications. (Use emojis as often as you wish in your personal life.)

- Never use them with your boss or on legal or official documents.
- Emojis can be used in informal interoffice correspondence.
- A good general guideline is that if someone sends you an emoji, feel free to reply with an emoji.
- Emojis, like any image, can have a thousand different meanings, so be careful!
- Not all emojis come through on certain types of phones. Note that emojis don't always come through when texting someone with an Android or non-iPhone device.
- Don't become known as the Emoji King or Queen—not everyone wants to know if you are emoji chipper or sad each day.
- Emojis are fun but not a substitute for you taking the time to communicate in words:

 with your open.

Thinking before you post doesn't mean you can't have FUN . . . but it does mean that your success will skyrocket and you will not be taken down by an errant social media "missile."

## Respond and Comment

Using social media to build and enhance your business relationships will next level your success.

First of all, if all you do is post and expect others to respond and comment, you are just a "look at me" poster. Posting just to show off what you know is not a best practice. It is similar to going to a networking event and expecting everyone to just care about what you offer. Add some responses and comments to the posts of others. Engage in "conversations."

**TIP #1:** Guess who is looking at your social media? In addition to your friends, your boss could be looking. Think about when your boss would look at your social media; probably when evaluating for a promotion.

**TIP #2:** Life is easier if you are not Instagramming with your boss. Don't feel the compulsion to add your boss in all of your social media. Rule of thumb: If you wouldn't add your parents, don't add your boss.

Disagreeing with another person's tweet, text, or post can be like picking a fight and is not a recommended way to enhance your business relationships. Even if you are arguing online with friends and family you only see socially, your business associates will see it too.

On politics and controversial topics: While some of your business colleagues will express their political views, it is wise to stay away from such topics in terms of your original tweets, texts, and posts as well as in your responses.

# #Conscious Posting

As mentioned earlier, when you post something on social media, even for a few minutes, you have to consider the possibility that your post might now be "written in stone," in that someone could have already downloaded your post or taken a screen shot of it. This is exactly why every post you put up should be preceded by the conscious decision to post.

In particular, two lines that you do not want to cross are the ones that take you into oversharing or cyberbullying.

## Don't Overshare

A major consulting firm study shows that job applicants are actually turned down for jobs because of their social media profiles, but they may never know that it was their social media posting that cost them those jobs. It is highly likely that the profiles were on their personal accounts, so they thought they were fine. Meanwhile, Human Resource departments are known for checking out all the social media sites for potential job candidates.

A wise guideline to follow is not to put anything on the Internet that you don't want your future bosses, current clients, or potential clients to read.

In general, do not overshare online by posting

- Too often.
- Too many selfies.
- Inappropriate personal info.
- Boastful statuses.
- Complaining rants, especially those about work.
- Revealing or embarrassing photos of yourself.

# Don't Cyberbully

Bullying is the opposite of being polite, and there is no excuse for it. Take special note that while any type of bullying in the workplace is a problem, the online aspect of today's business world adds a venue where bullies do roam.

Steer completely clear of any posting that will make you look like a cyberbully. If you show up as a cyberbully online, whether in your personal or business accounts, you will be destroying your personal brand, and your success will plummet.

Even if you think you are right about an issue, NEVER

- Say online what you would not say to someone directly.
- Post cruel or mean remarks about others.
- Post rude statements for attention.
- Post revealing or embarrassing photos of others.

**TIP #1:** Words do hurt. And they can hurt your profile as they get shared around. Almost any social communication can become business communication, so beware!
**TIP #2:** Even if you're texting about someone else, what you say says something about you too.

# #Online Business Communication

Technology now gives us multiple ways to communicate, and each of these ways offers additional opportunities to interact. These communication methods also offer opportunities to next level your personal brand.

## Use Your Excellent Email Etiquette

Almost everyone has an inbox that is too full, so you want your emails to show up in the best possible way.

The most successful emails

- Have a clear subject line.
- Use a traditional font that is easy to read.
- Have concise content.
- Use language that is appropriately formal.
- Are not too informal; "Hey there, Ryan, what's happening?" is not appropriate
- Have no misspellings because they will stand out and not in a great way!
- Are spellchecked.
- Have no bad auto-corrects.
- Use a signature line to identify your company and include a contact phone number.

When you respond,

- Respond in a timely manner.
- Be careful about hitting Reply All. There are lots of stories about confidential information going out to "everyone" because Reply is so close to Reply All.

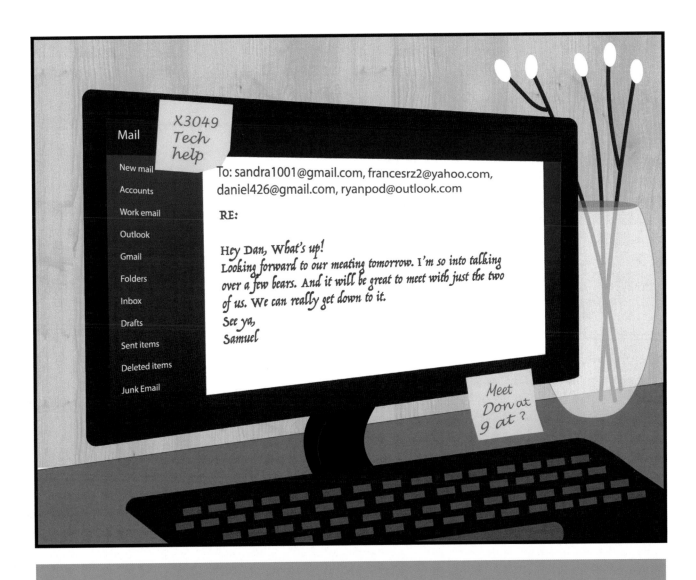

**TIP #1:** Don't become a "digital stalker" and send the same message via phone, email, and text. Too much.

**TIP #2:** If you send a text and the person responds by email—get the hint. For one thing, emails allow a more complex exploration of a given topic. Also, some people prefer email so they have an easy-to-find file of the communication.

### *Best Practices*

Don't blow someone off and just drop off the conversation. Give a reason for why you are no longer engaging. No one wants to feel dropped without a simple explanation. For example, if you are no longer interested in doing business with a particular person or company, just let them know. Say, "We have decided to go with another vendor. We will keep you in mind for the future." Or "We have decided to postpone our project at this time."

## Uplevel Your Text Messaging

When we think of text messaging, we often think in terms of personal communication. But its use in business is growing. Text messages are quick and direct, which encapsulates both their positive and negative sides. Because they are quick, it is easy to make communication errors. Because they are direct, it is a challenge to get the right tone for your messages.

You don't want to use text messaging as your primary mode of business communication, but it does have a place in business today.

Here are some other #Next Level Manners tips for business text messaging:

- First and foremost, limit your business texting to reasonable hours. No one wants to get your business text at 2 a.m.
- Keep your texts to one or two sentences long.
- On the other end of things, don't send one-word texts.
- Because you have a small space for your message, make the content targeted and relevant.
- Watch your language: Texting moves so quickly, and it is easy to throw in an abbreviation or general language that you will regret later.
- It is also very easy to make spelling and grammar errors, which will affect your brand. Make sure your phone is set up for spell check.
- Watch your tone: There is a tendency to use incomplete sentences while texting—don't. You don't want to give off a curt or abrupt vibe.
- Check the writing your voice to text feature creates. Sometimes it is not anything close to what you said.

- With business texts you may want to end with a signature. If the person will recognize you by your initials, that may be enough.
- If you use texting to change an appointment at the last minute, the person may not pick up the message. Last-minute changes are a phone situation.

# #Smart Phones & Video Conferencing

Smart phone conversations and video conference meetings are now part of the business landscape, and being able to successfully navigate these and other similar situations with your #Next Level Manners will boost your personal brand sky high. Remember, every communication opportunity offers a place to show up with manners, and leave with more success!

## Smart Phone Conversations

You likely have a smart phone. Use it to make your conversations smart too.

### *Hellos*

When calling, introduce yourself: "Hello, this is _____ (name) calling from _____ (business name)."

When leaving messages, if you get an answering service, speak slowly and clearly. Leave your name and phone number, even if you believe the person has them.

When answering the phone, give your name: "Hello, this is _____ (name)."

If you don't recognize the voice, say, "May I ask who is calling?" or "Whom am I speaking with?"

If answering someone else's phone, ask the person to call back and leave a voice mail message. This makes things easier for all involved and the message doesn't get lost.

### *Be Smart on Your Smart Phone*

Great phone etiquette will go a long way in promoting your brand and next leveling your career. Here are some tips:

- Smile through the phone—it will make a difference.
- Speak clearly and don't scream into your phone.

**TIP #1:** You may be starving, but please wait to eat lunch until you are off the phone. Talking and chewing don't have great chemistry. Would you want to hear crunching and chewing sounds from the other end of the phone?

**TIP #2:** Your work place may be casual, but eating and smacking your lips will turn off the person on the other end. Prove that you are in control of your world by eating your lunch on your time and not the customer's.

- Don't chew or drink while on the phone.
- Pay full attention to the call.
- Don't answer call-waiting while you're on the phone with someone else.
- Pick up the call only if you're available to talk. Decline the call if you don't want to take it at that time.
- When using the speaker phone feature, let the person you are talking to know you are putting him/her on speaker phone.
- There is nothing worse than putting someone on hold for a long time. If instead of putting the person on hold, you tell him/her you will call back, make sure you really do call back within a reasonable amount of time.
- If you want to put someone on hold, first ask them if it is okay to put them on hold.
- When you come back from a hold, thank the person for waiting.
- End your calls on a positive note: "Thank you for calling."

# Video Conferencing

Video conferencing is becoming more and more relevant. With services such as Skype, GoToMeeting, Onstream Webinars, and Google Hangouts, video conferencing can bring you face-to-face. Actually, since it's via our computers, it's really screen-to-screen.

Using your #Next Level Manners for your video conferencing is as important as using those manners in your in-person meetings.

Here are some specific tips for online meetings and webinars:

- Arrive a few minutes early and get settled in. Whether you are leading or attending the video conference, test your connections before the meeting to make sure everything goes smoothly on your end.
- Be prepared to introduce yourself.
- Speak clearly and with confidence.

**TIP #1:** Working remotely is not a license to be a video slob. Pretend the camera is a work colleague, make eye contact with the camera, and practice and use your best human skills in this cyberworld.

**TIP #2:** When you're on camera, watch what you wear and be conscious of your lighting and what's in the background. Don't eat while video conferencing.

- Put your phone on mute or silence when not speaking.
- Eliminate as much background noise as possible.
- If you are leading the meeting,
    - Finish on time or early.
    - Be prepared. "Spaces" in an online meeting can feel longer than if you are in-person.
    - Make sure you have a high quality, noise-cancelling headset to use.
- Specifically for online video meetings:
    - Maintain eye contact into the webcam.
    - Don't dress in complex patterns—they will be distracting on video.
    - Don't wear black or white—these colors do not do well on video.
    - Be careful about bright backlighting. It will turn you into a silhouette.
    - Consider your background. The background should look professional.

# Meet, Greet, & Network

Becoming a master networker, inside and outside your company, begins with the "meet & greet." The ability to introduce yourself to someone is key because the first impression is something you cannot easily undo. So learn how to give a great handshake and introduce yourself.

Beyond the very first impression, there are other very important factors to consider. Your body language speaks loudly, as do your actions, so be conscious of what you are "saying" here. Further, if you want to raise the bar on the impression you are making, be on time—a simple rule of thumb, one not so easy to accomplish, but so very important to those you could leave waiting. Additionally, there are many "presence" factors that can make or break the impression you make on others. For instance, great eye contact will win you points, while loudly chewing your gum will shave those points away. You can see how all of these points can add up to a great personal brand, or not.

When it comes to meeting people, there are some magic words—you will recognize them from your childhood, but the magic is still there. And "dressing for success" is the old-fashioned way of telling you to dress in a way that keeps you ready for a selfie that could go viral.

Finally, when meeting people, your "close" is a factor. Of course, how you wrap up the meeting itself is important, but your lasting impression will be affected, positively or negatively, by your follow-up. So, when you say you are going to do something for someone, do it. Now that is the good, solid type of follow-up that impresses everyone. Additionally, you have a secret weapon that will put your impression over the top: The ever-so-humble thank you note will send your personal brand into the stratosphere, right where you want it!

Knowing your way around the meet and greet basics will help you next level your networking and improve your personal brand within both your company and your field.

# Top Ten Guidelines *for meeting, greeting, & networking*

1. A good handshake matters.
2. Introductions open the door.
3. Your body language changes everything.
4. Actions speak louder than words. Do whatever follow-up you said you would do.
5. Be on TIME—no exceptions!
6. Face-to-face communication still matters, so having a presence matters too.
7. There are magic words that will open doors.
8. Looking great is good.
9. Be respectful of people with more authority.
10. Thank you notes are secret weapons in next leveling your career.

# #First Impressions

First Impressions get stamped into your personal brand. You can't take back your first impression, so make it a great one.

Essential impression factors are your handshake and your introduction.

## Your Handshake Matters

A good handshake is worth gold.

- Make it firm and confident with a solid grip.
- Maintain eye contact.
- Practice your handshakes. It only takes one friend.

No no no:

- No wet noodle handshakes.
- No endless handshakes. One shake is fine.
- No substitutes—no fist bumps or high fives instead of a real handshake.

## Introductions Open the Door

### *Introducing Yourself*

You want them to remember your name—so say your name clearly, with a strong but pleasant tone. "Hello, my name is Ashley Robinson." Adjust your volume: Don't roar but don't whisper either.

You might want to record your introduction with your phone and listen to how you sound.

**TIP #1:** There is no substitute for a handshake.
**TIP #2:** Guys, no bro hugging and no fist bumping at work meetings. It is one thing to work well together, but there are appropriate boundaries that communicate you are at work and not at the gym.

## Responding to an Introduction

If you are introduced to Luke Simmons for the first time, err on the formal side: Hello, Mr. Simmons. It is nice to meet you" instead of "Hey, Luke. How's it going?"

If you go by a nickname and are getting introduced, speak up. For instance, say, "Yes, my name is Abigail, but please call me Abby."

## Introducing Two People to Each Other

When introducing people to each other, try to mention a common interest they have. This will give them an easy way to continue the conversation. You can also mention something special about each person. Here are some more tips:

- Say the first and last names of each person.
- Speak clearly.
- Look at the person as you say his/her name.
- No need to do a two-way introduction. "Olivia Monaghan, Chase Jones, Chase Jones, Olivia Monaghan" will make your head spin.

## A Great Introduction Needs a Great Ending

At the end of your conversations, smile, shake hands, tell the person, "It was great to meet you," and go on your way.

Suggestions:

- Once you know someone's name, try to use it in your conversation. The use of the person's name will help you to remember it.
- Ask the person to spell his or her name. (This will be a silly request if the name is simple like Mia or Daniel. Use this tip only if the name is a complicated one.)
- Ask for a business card and look at the name written on it.
- Mentally make a connection between the person you're meeting and another person who has the same name.

# #Little Things Can Be Big Factors

If broken down, a simple meeting or greeting can be quite complex, and in many cases, what people think about you is ruled by a multitude of factors. The more we know about the many ways we can contribute to a great personal brand, the better. The following "little things" add up to be "big branding factors."

## Body Language Changes Everything

Posture matters. Whether on a conscious or subconscious level, people are picking up messages from your posture. Make sure you give them the right message: Sit and stand up straight, with your shoulders unslouched and relaxed. Good posture will feel good, look good, and get people to take notice of you.

## Actions Speak Louder Than Words

### *Positive Actions*

Here are two ways to make a positive impression:

- Stand up to greet people.
- Nod your acknowledgement as you listen to others. Showing your interest and respect with simple gestures like this creates great first impressions.

### *Negative Actions*

When people are talking to you, don't

- Fidget.
- Put your hands in your pockets.
- Cross your arms across your chest.
- Bow your head down and look at your feet.

**TIP #1:** Respect the personal space bubble.
**TIP #2:** Keep a breath mint or mouthwash in your desk.

- Look away.
- Cross your legs.
- Walk or lean into the personal space bubble of others (approximately 18 inches around the person).

Anything you do that signals disinterest will speak loudly, sometimes more loudly than what you actually say.

And of course, remember to put your phone away when meeting and greeting new people. For many of you, your phones are an extension of your right arm, so this may make you may feel naked and uncomfortable. Because you feel uncomfortable, you will need to be especially careful not to do the things mentioned in the negative list above.

### The Smile Factor

Adding a smile when you meet, greet, and network is great business etiquette and will add to your personal brand. A smile makes you look confident and friendly and takes away nervousness—for you and the people you are meeting.

Admittedly, it takes work to smile: It takes ten muscles to smile and one muscle to frown. So you can count smiling as part of your workout!

# #Raise the Bar Always!

Since your personal brand is such a key factor in your success, you naturally want it to represent you. Here are two ways you can give your brand more height.

## Timeliness Is an Asset

One of the best bar raisers for your personal brand is to be on time. Being on time says you respect the other person and your responsibilities. It is a courtesy that will be noticed and ultimately rewarded. There is no substitute for running on time.

Being on time will also ensure that you don't arrive to your meeting filled with left-over anxiety because you were running late. Getting to your destination on time means that you will be feeling confident and ready-to-go.

Suggestions:

- Plan extra time for travel, so you have some flexibility in case of circumstances beyond your control: for instance, parking issues, elevator problems, and traffic.
- When you calendar your meetings and appointments, make sure to allow for this "wiggle room."
- If you end up arriving at your destination early, you don't have to sit there idle. You can use your smart phone and stay productive.
- Confirm your meeting time and location the day before. It can be confusing if you don't have the exact address. For instance, a Starbucks at South Main and Hawthorne streets could be mistaken for other nearby Starbucks.
- If you are bad with directions or need some help being on time, you can use an on-demand transportation service like Uber or Lyft.
- If running late, inform the person you are meeting or the host of the event that you are running late and apologize upon arrival. (Call in case they do not read your text, and you don't want to text and drive anyway.)
- You can only be late with a particular person or group once.

**TIP #1:** No excuses for a millennial running late. You are mobilely productive.
**TIP #2:** Being on time is a habit. Start that habit now by being early and you'll soon find that you are very uncomfortable being late.

# Presence Is Huge

To exhibit next level presence, you have to be present, so be there—fully alert to the person you are meeting or meeting with. The way you show up makes a huge difference in how you are perceived and welcomed.

Other presence factors:

- Eye Contact:
  - In a conversation, a great way to show people that you are fully focused on them is to keep your eye contact consistent and tuned in.
  - Focus your eyes between the eyes, on the space above the nose.
  - As you speak to a group of people, try to create eye contact with each person in the group. This helps everyone feel included.

- Gum chewing or inappropriate crunch snacking will deduct from your "presence." Even if you are focused on others, the chewing or crunching will be distracting, it will not seem as if you are focused on them, and your "presence factor" will slip downhill.
- Show your respect for the other speaker by listening well.
- Reminder: Put that smart phone/tablet away! This does not mean in your hand. Put it in a pocket or purse. If it is handy, you will be tempted to look at it or answer its ring.

Networking presence:

- Specifically when networking, you will end up with a stronger presence if you help others connect. In contrast, the networker trying to make it all about him/herself will be quickly spotted, and judged accordingly. Nobody wants to talk to the attention hog.

- Business cards can extend your presence, so always have your business cards with you and handy. If they have your business card, people can remember and reach you.

- Your ability to make conversation at a networking event is key. Don't just take up space in the room. To next level your conversation skills:
    - Have a take.
    - Have a joke ready.
    - Be witty.
- Know what is going on in the world.
- Speak up. Don't leave a networking event without meeting at least 2 to 3 new people.

# #Extra Credit

Great etiquette can totally rock your personal brand. These "extra credit" factors will put you on track for your next level success.

## Some Magic Words

None of us likes other people putting words in our mouths . . . but there are some words that you don't want to resist. They can work magic and next level your personal branding in amazing ways. Here they are:

- Please.
- Thank you.
- You're welcome.
- Excuse me.

These words may sound old-fashioned, but they truly never go out of style. They may be obvious but they set you up for engagement.

Note: Leave the swearing at home. Actually, you might even consider taking the swearing out to the trash altogether. It is not the kind of language that will boost your personal brand or next level your success—in fact, it will most likely do the complete opposite.

## Looking Great Is Good

Most of your first impression is based on appearance, and a big part of this is based on how you dress and groom. In general, don't dress to the lowest common denominator in your workplace, a.k.a. the worst-dressed person in the office. Instead, dress to the level of the promotion you want.

Workplace dress codes and norms also vary by industry. Law and financial firms may still require suits, while tech companies like Google and Apple may have more casual dress codes. At either extreme, and all points in between, it is true that how you dress and present yourself will affect your career success.

In a CareerBuilder survey, 93 percent of executives said that an employee's style of dress affected his or her chance of a promotion. In many ways, your career is all about competition and job growth, so why not give yourself an advantage by looking your best?

The key here is to understand that what you wear and how you present yourself matter—and deeply affect your personal brand. So whatever you do, know what you are doing. Within the company's dress code, you will make choices. As long as you understand that your choices will make a difference in your career, you are free to make your choices.

So beyond your company's dress code, here are some guidelines to consider as you make your choices:

Choose to

- Wear industry-appropriate attire.
- Dress for the promotion you want.
- Be well-groomed.

At least think about it before you show up in

- Jeans.
- T-shirts. (If you are going to wear a t-shirt, at least make it a positive conversation starter.)

Really? The caution sign is flashing:

- Flip-flops
- Hoodies
- Workout clothes
- Very short skirts

- Sheer or revealing outfits
- Outfits that expose tattoos and/or body piercings
- Un-ironed, wrinkled clothes
- Brightly-colored hair, such as hair dyed pink or blue

Making an investment in your wardrobe is a smart career move. If you don't spend any money on your clothes you are probably not giving yourself many choices. Be careful about casual dress codes—they can be slippery slopes. Err on the side of over-dressing.

Showing up under-dressed can truly put a dent in your personal brand. Don't be afraid to ask about the dress code at any given meeting or event. Better to know than to guess. Remember too that regional dress codes can vary.

**TIP #1:** Dressing sharp, like the man on the left, should be a habit. If you're not comfortable doing it, then practice. It may start with having clothes you like in the closet.
**TIP #2:** A sign that you're too casual is not having to change your clothes to go to the gym.

Interview room H303

**TIP #1:** Dress to impress like the woman on the left.
**TIP #2:** If you don't invest in a wardrobe for yourself don't expect others to invest in you. Make sure the wardrobe commands respect, not just attention.

# #The Follow-up & Close

Everything has gone great with your meeting, greeting, and networking . . . so now it is time to wrap up the interactions with a positive spin. By following up and closing, you double the personal brand boost you have created. (This is not a scientific figure, but experiential evidence supports this claim.)

Follow-up comes in the form of accountability, and closing is all about having the codes to launch a great secret weapon—the thank you note.

## Accountability: Do What You Said You Would Do

Whether you are meeting new people or meeting with colleagues or clients, whether you are networking or working, make it a practice to follow through and do what you promised:

- If you promise a follow-up email, don't forget to send the email within 24 hours.
- When you tell someone in a meeting that you will send notes to everyone, do it.
- When you meet someone at a networking event and tell her that you will refer someone to him/her, do it.
- When you RSVP to an event or meeting, show up—and be there on time too.

To help you remember what your accountability "To Do's" are, repeat, to yourself or the group, the tasks you are taking responsibility for.

## Thank You Notes: Secret Weapons

We already touched on the importance of saying thank you. Expressing gratitude is quite simply, a powerful thing to do, and doing it verbally is great. But the cherry-on-top thank you is a handwritten note. They take literally 2 minutes to write. Try it and see what happens!

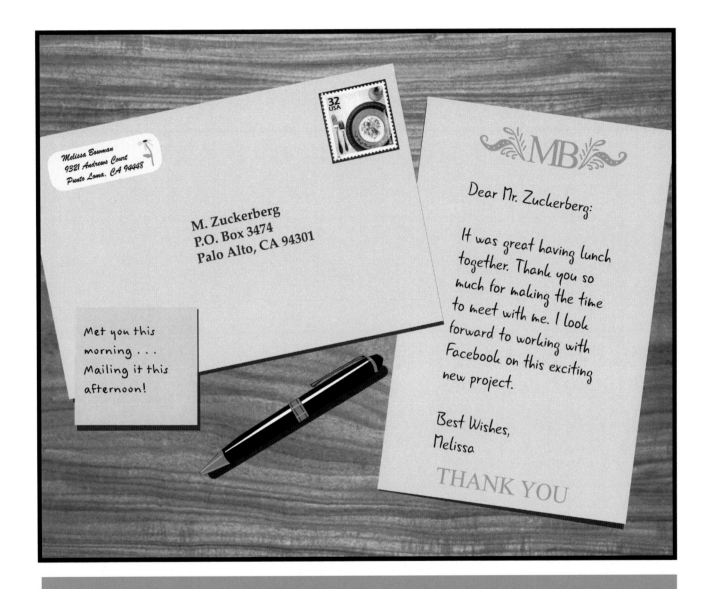

**TIP #1:** Take the medicine: Handwritten notes work. Texts are for kids—the handwritten note separates you from the pack and makes your brand shine.

**TIP #2:** Handwritten notes show you are someone who is organized enough to have stationery and thoughtful enough to take the extra time.

Online and brick-and-mortar retailers sell a wide variety of note cards. There are many types of designs to choose from, including classic designs and designs using specific themes, such as animals and sports, so you can choose one that shows your personality. This is an inexpensive investment in your brand.

While the champion thank you is the handwritten note, an email thank you can often step in, especially for job interviews being filled the same day. An email thank you has the advantage of quickness.

# Wine, Dine, & Impress

The business lunch or dinner is filled with potential: the chance to get to know your colleagues, clients, and even bosses on a different level. Just being outside of the office setting can be a plus. On the other hand, the business lunch or dinner is fraught with potential pitfalls, and you do not want to fall into any of them. Nothing is worse than a business meal gone bad.

One of the easiest things you can do to be prepared for wining and dining that will impress is to know your table setting. In this way, sitting down to a formal dinner does not have to be intimidating, and you will be able to use the right utensil at the right time and all will be good!

Additionally, your table behavior will be able to add up those "impress" points quickly if you have a few guidelines to show the way. At first it will seem like there are lots of rules, but once you open up to them, they will become second nature to you, and you will see how they create respect and courtesy at the table.

Naturally, a meal is not just a time to sit and eat. A meal is, in fact, a perfect venue for great conversations. The conversation guidelines shared in this section can, of course, be used in any type of meeting or social interaction, but are particularly useful for the dinner (or breakfast or lunch) meeting. As with most conversations, table conversation is a weave of listening and speaking, creating the best possible interaction.

In general, manners when dining are about grace and kindness, whether dining is for business or is a personal event. Remember that knowing your way through the wining and dining, in someone's home or in a restaurant, will leave a huge and positive impression, and add "brownie points" to your personal brand.

## Top Ten Guidelines    *for wining, dining, & impressing*

1. Know your table setting.
2. Use your utensils like a pro.
3. Eat and drink and be merry.
4. Score with the right table behavior.
5. Rock the conversation.
6. Focus the conversation on business.
7. Zap the electronic distractions.
8. Slay the other distractions.
9. The host should always pay.
10. Master the rules for a dinner party.

# #The Dining Table

When your colleagues or bosses think of you, do they think they can take you home or out for dinner? Why miss out on a great meal because you never learned which fork to use? For most millennials, growing up did not include formal family dinners every night. But now that you have a real job, you just might want to learn some table manners.

## Know Your Table Settings

If you know how a formal table is set, you will be in great shape for any variation of it. In this case, having rules about where everything goes on a table setting is good news. No matter where you go to eat, knowing the basics will serve you.

Follow the BMW Rule: bread plate to the left, meat in the middle, water and wine glasses to the right.

## Use Your Utensils Like a Pro

It may not be a huge issue if you use your entrée fork for your salad, but these dings can add up and lower your personal brand just far enough to put you in runner-up position for the next promotion. So why not take a minute and get this down? It will serve you the rest of your life.

General guidelines:

- Your small fork is for salads, appetizers, or desserts.
- Your big fork is for your entrée.
- Your teaspoon is for desserts and/or coffee/tea.

**TIP #1:** Learn what goes where on your place setting. You will reach your comfort zone.
**TIP #2:** Use your phone to take a picture of this place setting. This will give you quick and easy access to this valuable information.

- Your tablespoon is for your soup or noodle dishes (for twirling).
- Cut with a fork and knife—don't use fingers.
- Don't hold your fork like you are going to stab something.
- Cut as you go, one piece at a time, as you eat.

# #At the Table

Many times, job or promotion interviews are done over a business meal because it gives the interviewer a chance to see how you handle yourself through a meal. Whether you are being interviewed or not, it can be a big "tell" if you have great manners. It can also be a huge "tell" if instead of exhibiting #Next Level Manners, you do things like chew loudly with an open mouth and slurp your drink.

## Eat, Drink, & Be Merry

Keep these guidelines in mind at the business meal:

- People do not want to see or hear you chew.
- Chew quietly with small bites.
- Keep you mouth closed while you chew.
- Don't talk with your mouth full.
- Avoid crunchy, loud foods like raw carrots.
- Don't eat too fast.
- Pull off a bite-size piece of bread and use knife to spread a little butter on it. In other words, don't take a whole roll or big piece of bread, slap on a chunk of butter, and cram it in your mouth.
- Don't slurp the soup.
- Use a tablespoon and fork to swirl your noodles or pasta.
- Drinking:
  - No slurping.
  - No chugging.
  - No chewing ice.

# Wine and Alcohol

If the meeting is an interview, don't drink wine or alcohol at all. If it is a business meal, be wise about how much wine or alcohol you drink. No matter how much you drink, consider taking an Uber home. If the person you are with does not order wine or alcoholic drinks, you should follow suit.

# Table Behavior That Scores

We do more than just eat and drink at a dining table. Even though we have been present at the dining table since we were toddlers, there is a whole lot going on at the table that can be tricky to manage. The great thing is that the following guidelines will guide you right to an awesome personal brand and very sweet career success. Or you can be the one who starts food fights. Your choice.

Dining table guidelines:

- Your Napkin:
    - When you sit down at the table, place your napkin in your lap.
    - Put your napkin on your chair seat when excusing yourself during a meal.
    - Put your napkin on the table when the meal is finished.
    - Remember that your napkin is not a tissue—you know what I mean.
- Pass food counterclockwise.
- No reaching over people to get something—ask for whatever you need to be passed to you.
- Once you start using your utensils, don't put them on the table again. Put them on your plate.
- Never eat off another person's plate.

- No, No, No:
  - No elbows on the table.
  - No grooming at the table, including picking your teeth.
  - No combing your hair or putting on lipstick.
  - No hats on the table. In fact, hats off at the table.
  - No cell phones on the table.
- Push your chair in when you are leaving the table.

## Finger Foods

At receptions and events, finger foods are often passed around or set out on the buffet table. Finger foods can be delicious but "dangerous"—meaning difficult to eat gracefully. Why hosts pass around unshelled shrimp or falling-apart stuffed mushrooms, I will never understand. Even sushi can be difficult to eat gracefully. At a business event, some foods are best to let pass right on by.

Remember that business receptions and events are not really about the appetizers. You are there to next level your brand and career.

**TIP #1:** Enjoy the yummy appetizers, but don't try to make a meal out of them at a networking event. No one wants to see or hear what you are chewing. Don't hog the sushi; save some for the other guests! Don't show up starving.

**TIP #2:** Office parties are the informal testing ground for managers to judge you. Your first responsibility is to prove that you can handle the situation, not just the drinks. If you are getting louder and can't remember what the other person said, it's time for an Uber home.

# #Table Conversation

If you can find and refine your unique conversation style, you will ace the art of conversation. Having the skill to start conversations about topics ranging from sports to weather to movies to pets, even in business situations, is part of this art.

Conversation is a skill you can practice all the time, in business and socially, and the more you work the conversation muscle, the better you will be at using it to next level your success.

Although conversation skills were discussed in an earlier section, they pop up here again because, when dining, the conversation at the table is ever so important. In many ways, the conversation at a business meal is at least ten times more important than the meal itself.

## Listening

Being a good listener is the skill that will make you the best at conversation. This may seem ironic, but it is true. Be authentic and caring in your listening, and let the person know you are listening. Simple head nods and an occasional "interesting point" tell the speaker that you are engaged. Since people love to be listened to, you will be building your network—with your ears.

On the other hand, don't use the "I am being a good listener" excuse to stop you from truly engaging at your networking events. Yes, listen to others, but don't be a wallflower—engage!

## Speaking

### *Ice Breakers*

The "small talk" that comes before the business talk is actually not so small in terms of building your success. If you don't feel like a natural at small talk, prepare ice breakers ahead of time. Having them in your back pocket will allow you to relax and enjoy yourself, and when needed, there they are.

**TIP #1:** Know your audience; it is an art to be engaging in conversation without making people at the table uncomfortable. Don't convert, convince or corner your guest. Be a conversation starter not a conversation killer.

**TIP #2:** Sometimes it's better to talk about the weather than the daily newspaper headline. Even the colleagues you thought you knew well may surprise you with their politics.

Ice breakers often cover general topics such as sports, movies, and/or pets. Being fans of a particular sport or team can be very bonding, movies bring us together in shared stories, and who can't resist talking about his/her dog or cat?

Stay away from politics, salaries, sensitive health issues, and controversies. Remember, ice breakers should be designed to help avoid an awkwardness, not create one.

## *Work the Table*

Ask different people different questions. Do some research about the people you are meeting so you can prepare relevant questions, but don't make it seem like you are stalking someone by doing too much research and showing it off. Finally, be interested in the responses.

# #Focus the Business Conversation

First and foremost, remember that a business meal is not about the meal; it is about the business. As highlighted before, succeeding at the wining and dining as well as the small talk portions of the meeting is important. But don't neglect the business to be done and impressions to be made. Be ready to get into business mode.

## Lower the Distraction Level

An important element of business mode is focus, and the biggest obstacle to focus is being distracted, or being the distraction, at the table during a business meal. Remember, just because the wining and dining are added to the mix, this is still a business meeting. As in any business meeting, the other participants deserve your undivided attention.

So here and now, the following notes are not guidelines, they are rules. If you want your #Next Level Manners to boost your career success, you have to follow these rules . . . really.

### *Zap the Electronic Distractions*

The dining table at a business meal should be a Tech Free Zone. That simple.

### Don't Look

It is never ok to use a smart phone or tablet at the table during a meal, and this includes looking to see what messages, tweets, or posts have come in. Excuse yourself from the table if you really need to check your device.

A great addition to the "Don't Look" zone is to agree to take a break toward the end of the meal to check smart phones. But don't be silly and suggest this to the person who is interviewing you.

If you are waiting for an important call, give a heads up to the person/people at the table that you may have to excuse yourself to answer that call. For example, a "worth-interrupting" call might be a doctor's call you have been waiting for.

## Stop the Ring

Silence or turn off your smart phones or tablets at the table. If you want to be the one whose phone goes off in the middle of someone's turn to speak . . . well, then, I can't help you.

## *Slay the Other Distractions*

## Other People

Please don't be the person in the restaurant who is checking out people at other tables and ignoring his/her own table. Don't be the person talking over other people to talk to someone. Include them, change seats, or talk to the person later when you will not be distracting others.

## Timing

When you add the feature of a meal to a business meeting, timing is the factor that can be unpredictable and easily skew the schedule. Timing problems include restaurant delays such as slow service or logistical delays such as a tardy participant. Plan in the extra time so that you can accommodate any shifts to the schedule easily and with confidence.

**TIP #1:** You are not that important; the world will go on without you talking or texting during lunch.

**TIP #2:** Just checking your cell phone is checking out; you're losing your human audience just to avoid missing 45 minutes of your cyber audience.

### Hunger Equals Impatience

The impression you make, especially if you are presenting, will not be great if you have to rush into the restaurant looking to order right away because you came hungry. People might even be able to hear your stomach growling. Stop, in the name of your personal brand—don't be this person. The cure to this distraction is simple. Eat a snack on your way to the restaurant. In fact, you might want to have a stash of healthy snacks in your office and/or car.

## When You Are Hosting a Meeting

When you are the host at a business meal, you have some special responsibilities, and the overall success of the meeting will be on your shoulders. Don't just shrug it off—sit up tall and take the lead!

Here are some guidelines for being the most impressive host:

- Don't go starving even if it is your most favorite restaurant.
- Embrace your role as the host, and be proactive. For example, make sure people are seated where you want them—don't leave it to chance.
- To draw in both ends of the table, seat yourself in a middle seat.
- Don't switch seats if you have been given an assigned seat.
- For fun, play musical chairs for the dessert course. This moves people around and re-energizes the group.

# #Location Location Location

Many of your business meals will be at restaurants, but there are also business meals at the homes of colleagues, clients, and bosses. You are, of course, going to bring your #Next Level Manners to all your business meals, but there are also some specific things you can do in each of these circumstances.

## Eating @ Restaurants

If you are choosing the restaurant,

- Choose a restaurant you have been to before or ask a friend for a trusted recommendation.
- If going by recommendation, preview the spot in person if possible.
- Choose a restaurant that is not too noisy. The best way to know this is to visit the restaurant at the same time of day as your scheduled business lunch or dinner.
- Be conscious of your guests' allergies, sensitivities, and/or style of eating. For instance, don't take a vegetarian to a steak house.
- Be comfortable with the price point.

If you are hosting the business meal,

- Make the reservations.
- Call as far ahead as possible to make sure you get the time you want.
- If you don't want to call, Open Table is a great app for making reservations.
- Get there early so you can greet your guests.
- Hold doors, where appropriate, for your guests and for other patrons you cross paths with.

When ordering,

- Preview the menu online before your meeting.
- If you are the host, have a recommendation to suggest. This sets the price tone early. In fact, you can be assertive and order the appetizers for everyone. Don't be a democracy: A take-charge host is appreciated.

- If there is a host, follow the lead of your host. For instance, order the same number of courses as your host so you are not eating alone.
- Don't rush to order first, even if you are hungry.
- Avoid ordering foods that are messy to eat.
- Avoid ordering foods that get stuck in your teeth (i.e., broccoli).

During the meal,

- Wait for everyone to be served before you start eating.
- Treat the waitstaff with respect. How you treat the waitstaff at a restaurant carries significant weight in how others perceive you.
- Say "Thank you" when served.
- When getting the attention of your waiter/waitress, be respectful. Also be careful about scanning the restaurant to look for a waiter—don't ignore the people at your table.

When paying,

- If you asked for the meeting, pick up the check.
- Pay with grace and don't call attention to yourself while paying. You can discreetly give your waiter/waitress your credit card before the check even comes. Now that is picking up a check.
- You can also excuse yourself from the table and pay at the counter. This is a very classy way to pay.
- In situations where you are each paying your share, make sure to bring cash. It is also a good idea to have $100 (in tens or twenties) hidden in your wallet to bail you out of emergency situations.
- In either situation mentioned above, make sure to tip well. This shows respect for your waitstaff.
- If you are being treated to a meal, accept with grace. At the minimum, send an email thank you note to express your gratitude. And you know a handwritten thank you is the best.

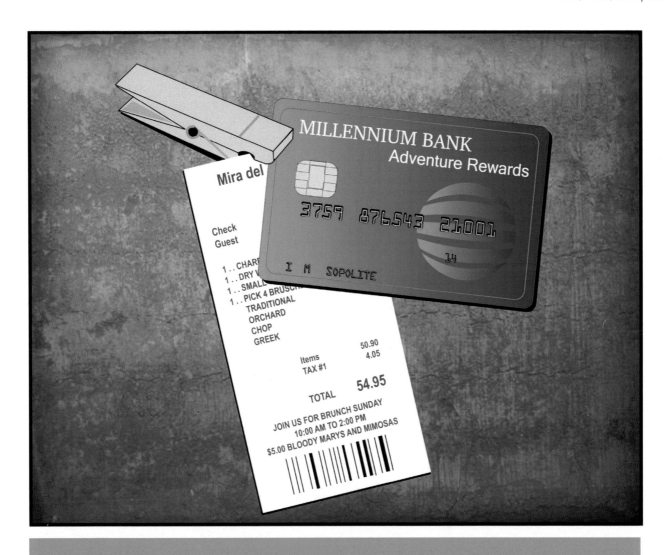

**TIP #1:** As the guest don't be a freeloader. It's always nice to offer your share even if it is politely refused.

**TIP #2:** Whoever asked should be prepared to pay, so pick a place where you are comfortable with the price. Set the tone and let your guests know what you are thinking of ordering, even as you let them order first. Pay discreetly and politely refuse their offer to pay.

# A Dinner Party @ Someone's House

When people invite you to their home for business dining, you are already receiving a compliment. No one wants to invite someone who is rude, disrespectful, and/or lacking in basic manners to their home. Your personal brand meter must be relatively high just to get this invitation. So what can you do to next level your manners for this occasion?

Here are some suggestions:

- Be on time.
- Offer to bring something to contribute to the meal.
- Bring something, whether your offer to bring something was accepted or not. In this case, don't bring a dish to add to the meal. Instead, bring a gift for the host(s), such as a nice bottle of wine, flowers, or nicely potted plant.
- Showing up hungry in a restaurant is not good, but showing up at someone's house needing to eat right away is rude and not easy to discreetly handle. Are you going to look around their kitchen for food? This is a big "Don't."
- If you like the food, compliment the chef—but if it is a business meeting, don't assume you can take pictures of the food for Instagram.
- Don't be the last one to leave and don't linger in the doorway.
- Send a thank you note or email after the event.

# Afterword

At the beginning of this book, we discussed how #Next Level Manners can make the people you interact with feel respected and acknowledged. I now challenge you to a sort of "experiment." Try some of the ideas in this book and see what happens. And with each new experiment, you will add to your #Next Level Success . . . and that will feel great.

You have worked hard every day to advance your career. You got an education and trained yourself and have done everything right. Now it's the little things that make a difference. You just spent an hour of your life reading this book to get skills that will help you for a lifetime and may be just the thing that makes a difference to next level your career.

The #Next Level Manners shared here are, of course, guidelines. You are the one who decides how to use the information and suggestions in this book. Your own experience will show you the way.

So I'm not telling you what to do, but I am telling you that you can totally next level this career thing by minding your business manners. Etiquette is an easy add and will definitively boost your brand, and success will follow. That simple.

# Sources

Page 5: "We can't say we are not distracted when on average we touch (tap, type, swipe, and click) our devices 2,617 times per day, according to a study by research firm Dscout." Dscout: www.dscout.com.

Page 8: "In CareerBuilder surveys, 18 percent of employers report the firing of employees for posting inappropriate material on social media. Employees also get fired for personal use of the Internet during working hours. According to CareerBuilder, 28 percent of employers have fired workers for this reason." CareerBuilder: www.careerbuilder.com.

Page 38: "In a CareerBuilder survey, 93 percent of executives said that an employee's style of dress affected his or her chance of a promotion." CareerBuilder: www.careerbuilder.com.

# Credits

Most emojis courtesy of EmojiOne, www.emojione.com. Social media emojis courtesy of Dreamstale, www.dreamstale.com. All other emojis created by Sarah Lane.

**Pattern credits for illustrations:**

Cover: Watercolor Background Design by Aviya Benmelech Chovav, http://www.freepik.com/free-vector/watercolor-background-design_942623.htm#term=yellow&page=2&position=24

P. 7: Purty Wood by Richard Tabor, https://www.toptal.com/designers/subtlepatterns/page/24/

P. 11: Fresh Snow by Kerstkaarten, https://www.toptal.com/designers/subtlepatterns/page/6/

P. 15: Wood Board Wood Grain, https://freestocktextures.com/texture/wood-board-wood-grain,78.html

P. 23: Purty Wood by Richard Tabor, https://www.toptal.com/designers/subtlepatterns/page/24/; Leaves Pattern Design by BSGStudio, http://all-free-download.com/free-vector/

download/leaves-pattern-design-in-symmetric-arrangement_6825371.html

P. 31: Subtle Grey by Haris Šumić, https://www.toptal.com/designers/subtlepatterns/page/15/

P. 34: Retina Wood, by Atle Mo, https://www.toptal.com/designers/subtlepatterns/page/16/

P 40: Abstract Swirly Vector Pattern, by lavarmsg, https://www.vecteezy.com/vector-art/83199-abstract-swirly-pattern-vector

P. 41: Grungy Natural Beige Pattern, http://backgrounds.mysitemyway.com/background/grungy-natural-beige-patterns-5/

P. 43: Wood Grain Clipart, https://thetomatos.com/free-clipart-18546/

P. 53: Retina Wood, by Atle Mo, https://www.toptal.com/designers/subtlepatterns/page/16/; Lace Texture Vector by sunshine-91, https://www.vecteezy.com/vector-art/103735-lace-texture-vector

P. 55: Rice Paper Texture, by Kjpargeter - Freepik.com, http://www.freepik.com/free-vector/nice-paper-texture_901287.htm

P. 59: Wood Pattern, by Alexey Usoltsev, https://www.toptal.com/designers/subtlepatterns/page/30/

P. 63: Copper Pattern, by dyrk.wyst, https://www.pinterest.com/pin/448248969134404911/

Made in the USA
Columbia, SC
06 August 2020